The Self-Publishing Skill Series

Book Descriptions That Sell

Learn Killer Strategies for Writing Book Descriptions to Make Bestselling Books!

Dr. Gary Webb

PublishingPoints
Author Services

Dalton, Georgia

2016

PublishingPoints
Author Services

Disclaimer

upon any purchase from the company. While the author and publisher take no responsibility for the business practices of these companies and or the performance of any product or service, the author or publisher has used the product or service and makes a recommendation in good faith based on that experience.

Leave a Review as Soon as You Finish!

I hope you enjoy and benefit from this book. If so, please help others to learn more about this subject. The best way is word of mouth to your friends, but another way can reach even more. If you will write a simple review on Amazon, you can help hundreds or perhaps thousands of other readers to make their buying decision. Like you, they worked hard for every penny they spend on books. It is important to match the best books with the right readers. With the information and encouragement you provide, readers can take action right away.

You can share anything you think will be useful, but here are a few suggestions:

   ✓   Why you decided to buy or read this book?

   ✓   What did you like most about this book?

   ✓   What makes this book different from others you have read?

   ✓   Did it give you practical ways to apply the information it provides? If so, share what you are going to be doing differently because you read it.

✓   What kinds of readers would benefit most reading this book?

Immediately after reading is the best time to leave a review.

Check Out Other Books By This Author

Christian Topics

Free Indeed: A Devotional for Saints Who Still Struggle with Sin

The Meaning of the Cross: Its Impact on Your Life

Weight Loss

Lasting Weight Loss: What Have You Got to Lose?

Your 5 Keys to Keeping It Off: Answers that Work

Self-Publishing

Prepare! Publish Promote Books 1-3

Book Reviews That Sell: Discover the Secrets of Getting a Boatload of Great Reviews

Foreword

This book is written for new nonfiction authors, but it includes material that can be useful to fiction writers too. It includes one appendix showing the differences that must be incorporated into novels and other fiction books.

Although most of the information provided in the book is useful for preparing descriptions for other online retailers and for the back covers of printed books, I have written it with the Amazon platform in mind. Once you have your book on Amazon, you should be able to send it to other sites just as easily.

If you need more help with writing a nonfiction book description, please contact me at gary@mgwebb.net. Be prepared to share your best efforts at writing the description, so I can help you improve it.

GARY WEBB
http://www.mgwebb.net

Introduction

"A great book description follows the old marketing mantra of 'create a problem, be the solution.'" The book and author shouldn't be mentioned until the very end of the book description. The book description shouldn't just describe the book. It should describe a problem and tap into core human desires in the process and pitch the book as the solution to that problem." -- Buck Flogging of "Buck Books" fame.

Over the past three years, I've written hundreds of book descriptions for other authors. Some of them were easy because the book itself was a delight to read. Its subject was interesting, and the content was exceptional. The best way to have a great book description is to write a fantastic book. Do that, and it will be much easier to convince readers that your book is something they should buy.

The most important part of writing book descriptions

The single most important thing to keep in mind when writing a book description is its purpose. I will repeat this often. A book description is written to convince potential readers to buy the book. All book descriptions offer information on the contents of the book. More important than that knowledge is the way a description motivates readers to click the orange buy button on the Amazon book details page.

Your book may instruct readers in how to develop a skill. Do not emphasize only what its readers will learn; help them see the value of having that new skill. Your book may show them how to do something. Your description should show them ways their lives will be better because of the new ability gained by reading the book.

The book you are reading isn't only how to write better book descriptions. It concerns how to write book descriptions that will sell more books. My description should focus on assuring readers that the information in this book will help them sell more books. Few authors want to write better book descriptions unless it increases their income.

It's an Advertisement, Not a Review

A successful book description is a powerful piece of advertising sales copy. Although it gives information on the book, selling more books is the goal. Comments on the writing style are valuable only if they motivate the buyer to action. Comparisons of your book to the work of famous authors is only to capture interest of those buyers and sell more books. The worst-written book descriptions contain good information on the book. But, they often fail by leaving readers undecided on what the book can do to improve their lives. The book description didn't sell the book!

An effective book description is not a book summary. It makes people want to read the book. Such a description resembles a movie trailer on television. It doesn't tell everything in the movie. Instead, it teases viewers to go to a theater, buy a ticket, and watch the whole film.

Don't yield to the temptation to tell potential readers too much. Give them the reasons and feelings that move them to buy and read the book. How? Let's look at how various kinds of books need different descriptions.

For a nonfiction book, you must show the problem the book will resolve. A description for a fiction book should stir the emotions to help readers sense the entertainment, enjoyment, or insightful change of perspective that the book produces. For example, the description may raise a puzzling question on the main character-- one that begs for an answer only to be found inside the book.

Step 1: Know Your Readers - Their Needs, Problems, Fears, and Dreams

The first step in exceeding your customer's expectations is to know those expectations. -- Roy H. Williams

When you know who your customers are, that can give you an edge on the competition. -- Alain Bouchard

◆———◆◆———◆———◆◆———◆

The first thing you will need to understand when writing better book descriptions is your audience. You needed that information while writing the book itself, but if you didn't do your research then, do it now in these final stages of setting up your sales platform.

Before you write the first sentence of your book description, you should clarify the reading audience you are seeking to persuade to buy your book.

Who are your reader/buyers and what are their needs, problems, fears, hopes, and dreams? These people want positive changes in their lives. If your book can deliver those changes, they want it.

Writing a book description resembles fishing. Not fishing with a cast net, but fly-fishing! A fly fisherman knows the exact kinds of flies are most appealing to the fish they are seeking to catch. They know how to manipulate the fly so it teases the fish closer and closer until it can resist no longer. As a result, the fish bites, and the fisherman smiles with satisfaction. Great skill is required through practice and experience dealing with those glittering fish beneath the surface of the rushing stream.

You need to understand your prospective readers just as the fly fisherman understands the fish he catches. Since you aren't writing the book itself you need quick and easy ways to better understand the readers who might enjoy your book.

Two Easy Ways To Get Information on Readers

One method to understand your readers is to find books like yours and read their reviews. If the books are similar, those readers will include your potential reading audience. These reviews will show what readers hoped to find in those books. The reviews will describe what these readers liked best and what disappointed them. As you read each review, take notes. List specific needs these readers were trying to meet when they bought the book.

Book reviews are a reflection on how well a book met the readers' expectations. Those expectations come from the title, book cover, and from the description on the sales page. If the reviewer feels cheated with false information, his comments will show it. But, if the book delivers on reader expectations, the review will often point out what content or style factors readers appreciated most.

If your book is strong in the same areas most praised by readers of similar books, you should include those points in your description. Why? Because that is the information readers are hoping to find when buying books in your niche.

Another way to get good information on your potential readers is to read blogs or forums on your topic. Search for them on Google or use social media such as Facebook to find online meeting places for people interested in your topic. There, you can eavesdrop on your prospective readers as they ask questions and discuss possible solutions. These people are searching for answers. I hope your book provides the information they need.

These Facebook groups can become resources of shared information that could be added to your book itself. In addition, you can befriend group members and later invite them to write reviews of your book (another way to sell more books).

These two methods for understanding your readers are simple but effective ways to research your audience before writing a book. They don't need technical data analysis skills to help you understand your audience. These techniques might help you narrow your topic to the things people are seeking to understand instead of giving answers to questions no one is asking.

Action Steps:

1) Make a list to describe the typical reader for your book. Picture that reader in your mind. What gender is this reader? What age or education level? Kind of job? Income? Most common interests and hobbies? Favorite types of TV shows or movies? Favorite foods? Car or truck? Be as specific as you can because it will help you know who will read your description.

2) List three people you know who might resemble your typical reader. Call them and ask them what they most want to find

in a book on _____ (your topic). Write those items in a list because they will help with Step 2.

Step 2: Know Your Book and How Its Benefits Fulfill Reader Expectations

I do want to work on writing, because writing's a skill. Writing is something that you can train yourself to know better. To know yourself better. And it's intimidating as hell. -- Kristen Stewart

You need to know your book and what it offers for your readers. What does your book offer that can rock your reader's world by meeting their needs? Does it offer benefits that your competitors have overlooked or neglected? What makes your book so special?

Before you write your ideas for a book description, it might be good to skim through your book. Take notes. Read through the eyes of the imaginary reader you identified in Step 1. What things in the book might such a reader most enjoy? Put those things in your notes.

Find the Problem Your Reader is Trying to Solve

Your book should try to answer questions your reader is asking. While going through the book you might imagine the feelings your readers have on the topic. For example, you could have a book topic on managing the stresses of overworking. Does your book vividly show the problem, so it relates well to your typical reader? Could your reader say you have given actionable solutions for his or her problem?

What are the desires, the fears, or the frustrations your book identifies and solves. You need to consider how to magnify the seriousness of the problem in your description in one or two sentences. The consequences of not solving the problem are important. Explaining the results of not taking action can build a stronger urgency to buy your book.

The Reader's Big Question: What's in It for Me?

"What's in it for me?" is the one question every salesman must answer for every customer. As the marketer for your self-publishing business, you must do the same.

Your book description is a quick sales pitch. In order for that pitch to work, it must be custom designed for the reader you are trying to reach with your book.

Regardless of what genre of book you have written, it should deliver benefits to the reader. Without looking at your book, what benefits does it offer? What benefits are shared in your book that might not be easily found elsewhere? Each book class presents different advantages to readers.

Novels or other narrative books should always entertain. They may inspire or encourage, but they should always help the reader enjoy the time spent with the characters in the book. The form of entertainment may vary. Yours might include humor or horror, biography, or fantasy. The story could be a James Patterson thriller or a J.K. Rowling adventure with Harry Potter. Other readers want a romantic comedy or a children's fairy tale.

Self-help or how-to books should always educate the reader in new skills to carry out tasks they value. Whether you are building a storage shed or overcoming a habit, the reader should see how his goals are better achieved with the help of this book. The popular "Dummies" series of books are good examples of these. Books on getting out of debt, raising successful children, making good grades, getting a better job, or losing 30 pounds in three months are often bestsellers because they engage readers with the "how-to" skills that match their needs.

Business and productivity books empower their readers with money-making skills. A book's description of business should paint dollar signs in the mind of the reader. These books are empowering with attitudinal changes such as those written by Tony Robbins. Others are filled with financial strategies such as those by Dave Ramsey.

Reference books should enlighten the reader with easy-to-find information when needed. The author should seek to find and explain the category of knowledge his readers can expect to find within the pages of his writing. This category isn't limited to encyclopedias or dictionaries.

It may include books tell "everything you need to know about xxx." Many of these books will advertise themselves as the "ultimate" guide to whatever.

Be sure you write your description with such benefits in mind. Be as specific as possible on benefits you are offering. Examples written with imaginary composite characters can do the trick for many books. Use creativity to show what your book says that will be most helpful to your readers.

Action Steps:

1)   As you skim through your book, list several phrases that finish this sentence: "People should want to read this book because it will help them..."

2)   In another list, write out the problems your book will solve for those who read it.   (This may include items from the first list. It is a different way to look at your book contents).

3)   List one thing your readers will remember best in your book a week after they finish reading it.

Step 3: Know Your Competition

It is nice to have valid competition; it pushes you to do better. -- Gianni Versace

Study the Descriptions of Best-Selling Books

Many best-selling books succeed in spite of their book descriptions. They have great sales because of their title, cover, author, or special pricing. If these factors are strong enough the reader won't bother looking at descriptions, reviews, the "Look inside" feature or anywhere else. They will click the "Buy now with 1-Click" button with no need for more convincing.

You should be realistic in your expectations. An excellent book description is only part of the recipe for successful self-publishing.

One of the best ways to learn how to write a description for your book is to study ones written for the best-selling books in the same category. You should give a close look at those resembling yours. For example, if your book is about deer hunting, put those two words into the Amazon search bar.

In this way, Amazon becomes your best friend to find books competing with your own. Amazon will display books on deer hunting after you select your topic. The books show up in the order of how often they have matched the keyword(s) in your search. This isn't the same as a best-seller list. But, it helps you find the best-selling books like your own. If you select any of these books, you will go to its details page. There, you can scroll to the categories for the book, choose one, and find out the other best-selling books in its category.

Once you have found the best-selling books in the category, you can study how their book descriptions are written. Most of the time, best-selling books have average or above average book descriptions. Sometimes, a great-looking cover and a hot title boosted the sales far more than reviews or a strong description.

Inspect the descriptions for these top ranking books. Find a few of the best descriptions -- ones that stir your interest in that book. Examine those descriptions to see what parts most appeal to you. Is it the headline? That first paragraph? The list of benefits? The call to action? Are there particular power words that stir your interest? Whatever you find most compelling will give you clues on what you should include in your own description.

Pay attention to the wording for the headlines, and first sentences, and the formatting of paragraphs you find most appealing.

Notice any indicators showing the exact audience the author is seeking to reach. What images and needs or desires does the author use to stir the emotions of his potential readers? What age group might be most interested in buying that book? Why?

Compare the book descriptions of a few best-selling books in your category with the reviews they have received. Focus your attention on the negative reviews. What disappointed those readers? Did that description promise more than the book delivered? That's one mistake you can avoid! Could the author have avoided those disappointments with a more exact or more complete book description?

What to Do After Looking Over the Competition

List things you think readers want to see in your description. What might turn them off? Try to focus on what might get the juices flowing for your typical customer.

I'm assuming your book is finished. If that is so, I'm arriving late. I hope your readers were on your mind before you wrote the first word of your book. If your book is completed, I recommend that you read it through the eyes of a customer.   With a printed manuscript, you can scribble right on the paper.   If you read the description on your computer or another device, you can take notes with your notepad or TextEdit app.   Here are two things you must include in your notes:

First, record thoughts about the person to be helped by each segment or chapter of the book.   Note that person's interests, hobbies, problems, goals, and needs.

Second, what kinds of benefits does your book offer for the person described in #1?   You should make a list.   The list should more than boring facts or information about the contents of the book. Instead, it should tell how this book might change the lives of your readers for the better. If it doesn't do that, write a better book! If it will make no one's life better when they read it, no one should buy it!

Once you know the people you are trying to reach and how your book can change their lives, the hardest part of the book description is done.

Now is the time to move into writing those high-converting (sales-producing) book descriptions. In the next few chapters, we will try to answer your potential reader's biggest question about your book: "What's in it for me?" If we can answer this question, you may have a bestseller on your hands.

Writing a good description should never be treated as unimportant.

WOE TO THE AUTHORS WHO GIVE THEIR BEST TO PRODUCE A QUALITY BOOK BUT ONLY A MOMENT FOR ITS DESCRIPTION.

Authors who spend too little time producing a strong book description seldom become best-selling authors. Many self-published authors have great confidence in the value of the book, but they fail to help readers share that confidence and WANT their book! Unless readers want your book more than they want the money in their billfold, you don't have a sale.

Some authors cannot write a book description for their own books. Knowing the value of descriptions for their sales, many of these authors hire someone else to do it for them. I have included a few of these freelance description writers in Appendix C.

Give Your Credentials

One way of dealing with competition is to give your credentials for writing on your topic. These need not be academic degrees or professional licenses. Maybe you have had the same problem as your readers, but you've found a solution that works. That makes you qualified to write on the answers you have found. Your testimony of struggle followed by success can be very effective. It can give readers hope because they want to find out what worked for you. It might work for them too.

You could give examples of people who have adopted your method or technique, with winning results. You might even quote one of them. This is called social proof, and it can convince readers that your ideas could work for them.

Action Steps:

1) Find three books on Amazon that you consider like yours.

2) Read each book's table of contents. List things your book offers that are not included in those books. If the books have any negative reviews, give them a close look. Do any of the reviewers' comments show problems with those books that are not true about yours? Make sure your description points out these strengths!

3) What are the experiences, credentials, successes or failures that have contributed to you being an expert on the subject of your book?

4) Skim the descriptions of some high-ranking books in your category. What positive features of those descriptions are true of your book? What are a few keywords you notice that can be included in your book description?

Step 4: Know How Readers Find Books to Buy.

Many of us spend too much time trying to find readers for our books instead of helping readers find our books. -- Dr. Gary Webb

As of this writing, Amazon has 4,211,146 books in its Kindle store and far more in its print books. That means you can find books on any topic you can imagine. But, from an author's point of view, it can be frightening. It can be impossible for a reader to find your one book among so many.

Amazon has been so successful because it is organized to help buyers find the products they want. This applies to book buyers too.

Before we go any further, let's try to understand how readers will find your book. They have several possible ways, so you should understand all of them.

Several years ago, Smashwords did a survey on how readers find books to buy. Here is a quick summary of their findings. Readers discover books by:

1. Using the "recommendations from fellow readers on online message forums, blogs and message boards."

2. Looking for their favorite authors.

3. Random browsing of book covers within a category.

4. Looking at reviews of books whose covers were interesting.

5. Reading free books, then buying other books from those authors that were good.

6. Looking at paper books in bookstores, then going online to buy the ebook.

7. Sampling inside the book at random until finding something that grabs them.

8. Searching for words and phrases related to a subject that interests them.

9. Looking at the bestseller lists.

10. Recommendations from the retailer's "Customers Who Bought This Item Also Bought" feature.

Since I'm not a famous author, I cannot rely on a large following of people searching for my latest release. That may be true for you too unless you are a novelist such as James Patterson or a nonfiction author like Steve Scott. If we keep writing more books and promoting them well, we will get there. But, in the meantime, most of us need to help readers find our books in other ways.

We can do our best to get a good book cover -- the best we can afford. But, unless you are a great cover designer, at least get a $5 one from fiverr.com. You can get good ones from the designers I mention in Appendix C. I have used none of them, but several of my friends recommended these.

If you can spring for more cash, get a true, professional cover for under $200 at archangelinc.com. When readers see a hot cover with an enticing title, they will look at the description to see what the book offers.

Descriptions can play another role in helping modern readers find books. The contents of your book description are indexed by Amazon. If your book description includes often used keywords, the Amazon search bar can direct many readers to your book detail page. Learn more about using keywords in my book, **Prepare! Publish! Promote! Book 1** or in the references included in the bibliography to this book.

How Do Readers Shop for Books?

Let me state my assumptions on readers. Book buyers seldom "browse" through a random list of books to see if they can find one to read. **They don't skip from one book page to the next on Amazon or another online book retailer, hoping to find something interesting.** That isn't how the sites like Amazon are organized.

The equivalent is a lady walking the aisle at Books-A-Million® without knowing what sort of book she might buy. Seeing an interesting cover, she picks the book up for a moment, then looks for another one. That is a poor shopping strategy in a bookstore at the mall, but even worse with Amazon.

Physical bookstores are organized by categories and styles. The stores have other sections or displays for particular authors. Since Amazon has over four million Kindle books, it might take a long time to locate a book that interests you with a random approach. That is why Amazon has arranged their online store to make your job easier.

Amazon is structured to help readers find the kinds of books they want -- even to find THE book they want. Readers can search for a book because they enjoy a particular author. Or, they can explore books in a category and narrow it from there.

A few buyers might shop for a favorite book title. Maybe a friend told them about the book. Or, maybe they saw a movie based on the book, so they want to read the full story! Readers start their search with just a fragment of information, but Amazon has created a system to guide them toward books matching what they know.

Another assumption is that readers are motivated by personal needs when making their book-buying decisions. Not every reader has the same needs. But, all readers have needs. One buyer needs to find a new recipe for the approaching holidays. Another needs to learn how to repair a lawnmower motor.

You should ask yourself, "How does my book fit the needs of a particular group of readers?" Make sure your description convinces them they NEED this book.

Action Steps:
1) If you wanted to find a book like yours, how would you start looking? Would your search technique work? Would it make your book easy to find?

2) What search terms are in your book title, subtitle, or book description that might help a reader find your book? If your book seems hard to find, what words can you add to the

description to make it easier for your readers?

Step 5: Identity the Best Keywords

Some keywords will attract many "browsers" to look at your book. That isn't the goal of keywords. Well-chosen keywords will attract "buyers" instead of "browsers" to look at your book page.
-- Dr. Gary Webb

Keywords are important for authors to understand, at least in a basic way. "Keywords" are individual words or phrases that customers use to find products with a search engine. With a book on Amazon, keywords are used to help the reader navigate to the book detail page.

As authors, we can add keywords for our books into Amazon in several ways. The most common one is by including them in the book's title and/or subtitle. You can enter keywords into the KDP Bookshelf when a new book is added or when an author wants to test the effectiveness of some new keywords. The third way is to make sure that your book description is filled with great keywords.

Selecting high-quality, relevant keywords will help readers find your book page. That's when they can see the title and cover, look at the reviews, and read your full book description.

Keywords and Descriptions

Although I am not an authority on search engine optimization (SEO), I know well-selected keywords can increase the odds for buyers to find your book. Book descriptions can expand your chances to include keywords that will lead more readers to your book details page.

Choosing Great Keywords

One of the easiest ways to find keywords for your book description is trial-and-error experimentation with the Amazon search bar.

Enter words are associated with your topic or genre of book. Watch as you enter letters and words. Beneath that search bar, a drop-down box will appear with keywords frequently used by other readers in the past. The most often searched terms will appear closest to the top of the list.

When choosing search terms, you can trigger your imagination by asking yourself a few questions such as:

- What words will your target audience be most likely to use when searching Amazon?
- How high on the list of search words does each possibility appear?
- If your book is already published, does using of this word cause your book to show up on the first page of a search for the full phrase?

You also can use free online tools such as the Google Keyword Tool. I've recently used another free one called keywordtool.io. They try to sell their paid version which gives more information, but I do not need it. Look what I found when I looked up the term "book descriptions."

Search Terms ?	Keywords ?
book descriptions	book descriptions **that sell**
book descriptions	book descriptions **search**
book descriptions	book descriptions **and reviews**

I had not yet chosen a title for this book. When I used this tool, my choice became obvious. My only problem will be whether enough authors are looking for help on this topic. If they are, they should have no problem finding my book just from the title. If I had used another title, it would have been helpful to include the phrase "book descriptions that sell" in my book description.

Let me give you an example of how a reader might use the search bar to find one of my books. Imagine a new author searching for a book about getting more and better reviews. How would he do it?

If he understands how search bars work, he begins by selecting the department he wants to search. Looking at the list, he finds the Kindle Store. That's where he can find Kindle books. He selects that department and types "book reviews" into the search bar.

Grocery & Gourmet Food

Handmade

Health & Personal Care

Home & Kitchen

Home Services

Industrial & Scientific

✓ Kindle Store

Luggage & Travel Gear

Luxury Beauty

Magazine Subscriptions

By the time he has entered "book rev," the keywords show up below the search bar.

With those few letters, Amazon's search bar confirmed my title for my last book, **Book Reviews That Sell.** Since I did this screenshot after I had published the book, the drop-down menu shows my last name following "book reviews" for someone who wants to know more on book reviews. Amazon is guiding them right to my book! "Book reviews that sell" is a good keyword phrase to include in a book title or subtitle. It could be good to include in a book description.

Dr. Gary Webb

Kindle Store ▾	book rev|

Shopping History

book reviews

book revival press

book reviews on amazon

book reviews that sell ⬋

book reviews by readers

book reviews by me

book reviewer yellow pages

book reviews webb ⬋

book review reviews expert book

book review policy

If I typed the words "book reviews," the first phrase to appear is "book reviews on Amazon." I could have chosen that for my book title. But, the second one in the list is "book reviews that sell" -- the one I chose for my book title.

You can trigger your imagination by asking yourself questions

such as:

- What keywords will your target audience be most likely to use when searching Amazon for books on my chosen topic?

- How high on the list of search words will each possibility appear?
- Does this keyword cause your book to show up on the first page of a search for the full phrase?

You can use free online tools such as the Google Keyword Tool. In a recent search, I used another free tool called keywordtool.io. Look what I found when I looked up the term "book descriptions."

Search Terms ?	Keywords ?
book descriptions	book descriptions **that sell**
book descriptions	book descriptions **search**
book descriptions	book descriptions **and reviews**

My book title ranked #1 on this list of keywords. The best place for a keyword is in your title. My only problem will be whether enough authors are looking for help in this topic. If they are, they should have no problem finding my book just from the title.

Using keywords in a book description is an art form itself. Many keyword terms can be hard to use in your sentences.

As you are writing your description, you should seek to use keywords as naturally as possible. Awkward writing just to use a word will weaken the power of the description to sell books.

One way to use keywords is by attaching them to the elements of the book structure. With a fiction book, for example, you can use keywords that describe the character roles (strong female warrior, mysterious hermit). It could be a character type (farmer, veteran, divorced, single mom). It could be a setting which positions it in time and place (colonial America, post-Civil War South). You might refer to plot themes such as revenge and forgiveness or passionate romance. Fiction often has a special tone, so you could use a description word for that (dystopian, horror, light-hearted). See Appendix B to see more differences in writing fiction descriptions.

Nonfiction books are easier because you can use keywords that describe the benefits. A book that explains how to build storage sheds might use keywords such as: "storage sheds," "DIY sheds," "storage buildings," or other similar terms.

To Increase Your Keyword or Category Options

One valuable tool for both categories and keywords is a thesaurus. Use it to find similar words that could expand your list of keywords. Many of the synonyms in the thesaurus may not be useful, but others are likely possibilities. Try them out in Amazon's search bar or with a keyword tool to see if they can find books like yours.

Ways to change keywords for Amazon.

You can use the book description to add as many keywords as you want for a book published on Amazon or most other online book retailers. Keywords should be blended into the sentences without being obvious to human readers. Computers can still find them because they do keyword searches without regard for how they are placed in sentences.

A few authors have added a list of keywords at the bottom of their description after their call to action. I consider this method tacky. But, I cannot say the approach is less effective when using the Amazon search bar.

The primary way to add keywords is through the KDP Bookshelf or Createspace Dashboard, not the book description. KDP allows you to use up to seven distinct keywords, separated by commas. KDP has no limit on the number of characters, either for an individual keyword or the total. That makes it easy for you to use what is called "long-tail keywords." Long-tail keywords use several words in a row before inserting a comma to separate them from the next word or group of words. Here is an example:

Search keywords (up to 7,) optional) (What's this?)

| book descriptions, book blurbs, writing more effective book descriptions for Amazon, |

(4 keywords left)

Notice that the words are grouped together and separated by commas. KDP allowed up to seven keywords, but I've only used three so far and have four keywords left. No matter how many words are between commas, they count as one keyword. That means your last keyword could be a long string of words you want to have included as search terms. It could be 20 high-rated keywords listed in no logical order. Since they are only being read by a computer searching through the list, it doesn't matter whether they make sense or not.

Createspace is much more rigid than KDP in its keyword limits. They will allow up to five keywords, separated by commas. But,

Createspace has another limit. They allow 25 characters or less per keyword. If you had one keyword with 28 characters, you couldn't enter all of it into their keyword box. One important little tip in the Createspace Dashboard is to not use spaces after commas. They are not needed, and each comma wastes one of those precious 25 characters. Since they have such a small box for keywords in the dashboard, you may need to depend on your book description even more for your paperback books.

In addition, Kindle Direct Publishing requires specific keywords if you place your book in certain categories.[1] Apparently, they believe using those categories alone could make it too hard to find books. Whatever!

Don't be afraid to change your KDP book description or your keywords often. These changes have can boost sales overnight.

Action Steps:
1) How does a book's category help a reader find the book? How does the category relate to your description? Do you repeat the category name within your description?

2) List 20 keywords that might help a reader find your book. Use tools such as Google's Keyword Tool or keywordtool.io. In fact, I recommend using the keywordtool.io because of its ease of use and how it quickly produces a long list of keywords. Remember, keywords are often phrases with several words, not just individual words. Make your list of 20 keywords, but then circle the top seven. These are the ones to use in your metadata in the KDP Bookshelf. Choose at least another five words or phrases to include in your book

description.

Step 6: How to Write a Book Description Headline

"Writing headlines is a specialty - there are outstanding writers who will tell you they couldn't write a headline to save their lives." -- Bill Walsh

---

A nonfiction book description has at least five parts.

- The headline
- The opening paragraph (with heading or subheading)
- The list of benefits
- A closing paragraph (with heading or subheading)
- A call to action.

We will cover all of this in the coming steps, beginning with the headline.

Making the Headline Pop!

Every effective book description includes a headline that captures the reader's interest.

At one time, Amazon made a larger portion of book descriptions visible without having to click the **"Read more"** tag. Today, little of the description shows at first glance. It is easy for a buyer to overlook the description completely . I have one solution that works well. I suggest that your first line say, **"BOOK DESCRIPTION:** in big bold lettering. If readers don't even notice the description, it won't matter how well it is written. This bold title makes sure they don't overlook your descriptions.

Just over a year ago, Amazon allowed the use of a bold, orange font for headlines and for emphasis. Amazon took that feature away because it gave a false impression that Amazon had written the book description. I now use bold fonts and underlining to emphasize key elements in the description.

Put your headline on the next line after BOOK DESCRIPTION -- still showing before the "Read more" link. Be sure your headline motivates readers to click to see what else you have to say. Your headline must stand out from the rest of the text. **Your headline should always have some special formatting to snag attention better.** I'll cover text formatting in step 11. Here is how the description for this book looks:

BOOK DESCRIPTION *Eye Catcher*   *Headline*

Do You Know the 12 Proven Steps To Write Book Descriptions to Make Your Book Sell?
Nonfiction authors often neglect being creative when writing book descriptions.
They imagine that the great content inside the book will make it a success. What a joke!

A few months back, I realized a problem with the way I wrote descriptions. I had been writing dozens of descriptions each week as a freelancer. During that time, I developed a habit of using the book title and subtitle as the headline. That is stupid! It doesn't serve the purpose of a headline!

Every headline should convince readers to think they NEED this book! It should begin to communicate urgency to buy this specific book NOW!

We have identified our readers -- understanding their needs, problems, fears, and dreams. Those key influencers should shape every part of our description, but especially the headline.

Headlines should magnify the need for a moment, but also promise help. The headline should have only one or two sentences.

Consider the headline of this book as it appears in Amazon. It is structured to cause authors to focus on what they don't know about book descriptions and to build some curiosity about that. It also appeals to their desire to increase the profitability of their book and gives an implied promise that they can make more money if they apply the 12-step process given by this book.

The headline must work together with the book title and subtitle to increase the sense of need and to offer hope for a solution. There are several ways to do that.

What should a nonfiction headline say?

It may contain a vivid promise. Readers who are businessmen might get excited when you say, "Make more money by working less." That should produce some curiosity! How can I do that? You need to buy the book to find out.

For an amateur fisherman, the headline might read, "Where to find your first trophy bass."

For those with bad sinus problems, the headline could read, "Follow these five practices and you'll never have another sinus headache!"

For married people who have lost the sizzle in their marriage, a headline like, "How to Get More Sex From Your Marriage Than You Can Handle" might make someone a bestselling author. Lots of people want to know the answers to that one! So, you need to promise a solution to one of your reader's problems. If that's why you wrote the book in the first place, there's no point keeping it a secret.

It might raise a thought-provoking question. "How Did More People Become Millionaires During The Last Recession Than In The Previous Five Years?" "What Do Warren Buffett And Mark Zuckerberg Have In Common That Made Them Both Rich?" "How Did Sarah Jameson Lose Over 100 Pounds In Less Than Six Months?" "How Can Wives Help Their Husbands Triple Their Income?" "What Are The Seven Sex Secrets That Can Make Marriage Better After 40?"

Sometimes, you'll want to raise a question like I did for the description of this book. I asked, "Do you know the 12 proven steps to write book descriptions to make your book sell?" I deliberately included the number "12." Even if a reader knows a good deal about book descriptions, they might ask themselves if they know everything they need to get more sales.

The headline can cite a shocking statistic to show the seriousness of the problem. Then, you can immediately picture a future without the problem. In this case, the headline might be more than one sentence. Try this one: "Eighty-Seven Percent Of Those Who Lose More Than 50 Pounds Will Gain It All Back Within Three Years. Don't Ignore The Six Strategies In This Book That Will Break That Pattern Forever!" Wouldn't you like to know the six strategies? If you did, you could write that book pretty quickly! What about, "The Seven Steps to Weight Loss that 62% of Americans Will Never Learn. Be One of the Few Who Know the Secret!"

You could use an example of someone who has overcome the problem and associate that victory with the content of your

book. For example, "Oprah Winfrey grew up in extreme poverty in Mississippi. Discover the secrets of her rise to riches." Or maybe, "Marie Osmond lost over 50 pounds in just a few months time. Her slim-down strategy included more than Jenny Craig." Notice how these leave you hanging because they make you form questions that are not answered in the description. The description doesn't give away the contents of the book. It just hints that you need to know what the book contains.

Why not ask a challenging question? For example, "Are You Fed Up with Work Conflicts That Are Costing You Money?" Or, "Can You Really Keep Dating The Same Guy If He Isn't Interested In Popping The Question?" Or maybe, "Are Your Sloppy Interview Skills Keeping You From Getting The Jobs You Deserve?" What about, "Is The Fear Of Rejection Keeping You From Closing More Deals?" Sometimes, these questions strike a nerve that makes the reader want a solution quicker. If they believe you understand the problem, it gives hope that you might have the answer.

Your headline can offer an incredible benefit. Try something like, "Five Ways to Double Your Sales Income This Year." Or you could try, "Using My Three Best Strategies, You Can Double Your Email List Within The Next Month." Or, "Twenty Way to Make an Extra $50,000 in the Next Six Months."

You can try the "How-To" hook. For example: "How to Make Her Want to Wake Up in Your Arms -- Even Though You Just Met." Or, "How to Shave Thousands Off the Price of Your Next New Car." Or, what about, "How to Land a 25-Pound Large-Mouth Bass on a Six Pound Line." Make sure you are very specific and sensory in what you are saying they will be able to do. Make your readers see and feel the benefits you are offering.

You may want to use the adversity challenge. This headline might say, "How to Break Your Weight-Lifting Record after Knee Surgery." Or, "How to Overcome the Worst Soil Conditions and Build the Best Lawn in Town." Maybe, "How to Qualify for a New Home Mortgage Three Years After Bankruptcy."

You could use a call to attention. This approach has the advantage of "qualifying" or targeting the kinds of readers who most need your book. It could say, "**Attention: Single Men Wanting to Attract Beautiful Women.**" Okay, I'll admit that doesn't trim the audience down much, but you get the idea. If you had a book for radio broadcasters, your call to attention might be: **Listen Up! Only Those Seeking Successful Broadcasting Careers Should Read This.**"

Whatever approach you use, make sure that your headline is **specific**. If possible include numbers or time periods to make the benefit of the book seem more tangible. It is always good to **relate** to your readers so they see that you have the same needs, problems, and ambitions they have. One way is with headlines that say, "Five Secrets to How I . . ." That is both specific and causes readers to relate to you as the author. Third, and most important, make sure you **grab their attention**. If you fail to get their attention with the headline, they are unlikely to read the rest of the description.

Examples of Killer Headlines

If you would like some good examples of the kinds of headlines that sell books, take a look at the headlines of the

National Inquirer or Globe newspapers. The headlines are outrageous, but they sell newspapers. They claim to have proof positive of the Loch Ness monster. They have the inside dirt on every Hollywood celebrity or national politician. They have bizarre prophecies from the Bible or Nostradamus. They play on scandals and tragedy, all in the name of selling more newspapers. Let me just say this. It works!

I'm not suggesting that you be dishonest about your book. That will come back at you in the form of bad reviews. However, the best headlines are extreme ways of saying things. Instead of having a headline that says "Jimmy Jones raised a big watermelon," you could have one that says, "Jimmy Jones tells how he grew his one hundred forty pound watermelon." The first book or article might say the same as the second, but which one sounds more interesting to you?

For fiction books, I would suggest a headline with penetrating, vivid words. One way is to start by identifying the genre of fiction with those power words. For example, "Like fingernails on a blackboard, this horrific suspense novel will make hairs stand up in places you didn't know you had any!" The point was simple, to produce an emotional reaction similar to what the reader might experience in the novel itself.

Other Great Ideas for Book Description Headlines.

This book is deliberately short. However, I do want those who need it to have some other options. Not all of them are easily found because they are not specifically about book descriptions. Recently I found a blog by AppSumo that gives some great tips for headlines to use in social media. It is one of the best concise resources I've found. You can find it at http://bit.ly/1Kg0hDU.

Headline Tools

I have a tool (a browser plugin) called **Headlinr Pro**. It cost me $27, but there is also a free version that's pretty good. You can get the free version at http://bit.ly/1I54ILg, or purchase the Pro one at http://bit.ly/1W6bYnp.

Another great tool is called **Headline Creator Pro**. It can be purchased for $17 at http://bit.ly/1Pc2oK8. That offer includes some additional bonuses to help with writing headlines. This tool is only available in Windows, not Mac. (**Note:** The same tool can help you create killer chapter titles).

Action Steps:

1) I listed a variety of ways to shape a headline. Which one would be the best fit for your type of book? How do you want your reader to feel after they read only the headline?

2) Write a basic headline for your description. Now re-write that same idea three different ways, trying to make sure it teases the reader into wanting to see what else the description says about the book.

3) Share your headline with a friend. Let him/her know that this is the headline for an article about your book. Ask them how they feel about that headline? Does it make them feel more or less interested in reading the book? Do they think there is a better way to word it? If so, how?

4) Using the free version of Headlinr, try to develop a list of possible headlines. Mix and match ideas. Be creative with possibilities that would capture reader attention.

Step 7: How to Write an Introductory Benefits Paragraph

"The book description shouldn't describe the book, it should describe a problem and tap into core human desires in the process and pitch the book as the solution to that problem." -- Buck Flogging (Matt Stone)

I confess, most of my earlier book descriptions discussed the book instead of the reader's needs. That is a bad mistake!

The purpose of the introductory benefits paragraph is to set the stage for a crisp presentation of the benefits of the book. Often it addresses how important the reader's problems are. The introductory paragraph is not a summary, but it leads the reader to appreciate the next part of the description -- a list of its benefits.

We should present the benefits for nonfiction and for fiction in different ways. Nonfiction descriptions are well suited to using bulleted lists, but fiction works better with a series of questions or strong statements that evoke the reader's emotions. I will present both types in the next step.

Do not write your description in the first person as the author. It should sound as though a publisher wrote it. The language should be simple enough for your typical reader to understand, but it should never sound like an author bragging on his book.

The First Sentence

Which two sentences of a book are hardest to perfect?   The first sentence; and the last.   The same is true of a book description. Your first sentence must be strong. If not, the rest of the description is wasted words. This sentence should be polished until it can draw readers into reading the sales points that follow. I suggest writing five or more versions of your opening sentence and reading each one aloud.   Narrow it to three sentences and ask someone else which sentence is stronger. But, you must make the final choice.

Don't overdo my suggestion, but I have a way to simplify writing the first sentence. This method could be used for a headline, but don't use the same formula for both headline and first sentence.

I often use what I call the "Get and Give" sentence.   In one sentence, you tell the reader what they will GET from the book and what they must GIVE to have it. You make the GET huge, but the GIVE easy.

 For example, "How would you like to double your income in just 30 days?" Doubling your income is a huge GET. Being able to do it in just 30 days makes the unknown solution sound easy. You can say the same thing without it being a question: "Double your income in just 30 days." Or, "Double your income in just three steps." I hope you see what I mean. It is the same formula used on many self-help magazine covers.

Demonstrate Credibility

Readers want to know why they should buy your book instead of your competition.   This is particularly true for nonfiction authors. That means you need to give credentials or experience to support your expertise in the subject matter. If you do not have that, you might include a couple of quick endorsement sentences from readers who have already benefited from reading your book(s). If you have written other books that have received recognition on bestseller lists or have received awards, these also support you having the necessary expertise readers are searching for.

Public recognition such as this is especially valuable for fiction authors to include in descriptions because degrees, licenses, or other common credentials are probably irrelevant to the content of your novels. Some exceptions might apply, however. If you are a police investigator who also writes crime stories, that motivates readers to see what you've got. If you are a professor of history at Harvard, some readers may be intrigued that you also write historical romance. Since you are a fiction writer, I'm sure you can use your imagination to convince readers of your exceptional competence to write within your genre.

Capture the mood

The emotional tone of your book description should match the mood of the book. If you've written a humorous book, the description should include humor. Don't just say that the book is hilarious. Show it with a joke -- maybe one taken from the book or one on the topic of the book. If your book is a self-help book, you should build optimism for the book's "five-step solution" to the problem. You might even give a tantalizing clue by selecting a single sentence from the book. As much as is possible, the description should give readers a taste of the feelings they will have as they read the book. Why? Because most buying decisions are made with the heart, not the head!

How to Magnify the Need

Sometimes, readers know they have a need, but they haven't become serious in seeking a solution. We need to show a vivid picture of the need. You can do that by showing how big the problem is or how difficult it can become. You could use a quotation from a recent news source or a series of terrible headlines from magazines about how great the need is.

Depending on your subject, you may add the power of statistics to show how overwhelming the problem is. For example, "Did you realize that 84 million Americans sleep less than five hours per night?" For someone who has a problem with sleep, such statistics make their problem appear worse and more difficult to overcome. That can trigger them to appreciate how valuable a book on that issue can be.

You might do it by telling a story that demonstrates how serious the issue is. This could be what I call a "composite story" which blends typical events together in a way that keeps the actual people anonymous.

Or, you can put your reader's biggest need or problem into the form of a question. For someone who is overworked, you might ask, "Do you come home too exhausted to spend any time with your kids, but you still can't afford a good vacation?" That should help your readers emotionally connect with the problem of being overworked, but underpaid. You could ask, "Are you working for a living, or living to work?" You could discuss a different part of the same problem, "Are you afraid to ask for a raise because it might cost you your job?" As an author, do you FEEL that problem your readers endure each day?

Use power words, words that strike a nerve. Describe the problem so vividly that the reader believes you understand their feelings completely. Then, they can have hope that you have the answer they need.

Emotion Words for Fiction Book Descriptions

Fictional books walk readers through an imaginary world with characters they love or hate, but cannot ignore. Use emotional power words in your description the way you did in writing the novel. Use those intense words to make your readers feel something. Use painful words, such as agonizing, biting, muscle ripping, nerve-twisting, or tortured. Or, use pleasant words, like sensual, refreshing, delicious, tantalizing, soothing or passionate. A Google search for "power words" will give you plenty of words to choose. For example, Jon Morrow listed 317 power words in a blog post at **http://boostblogtraffic.com/power-words/**. Obviously, many other sites will give you more. If you are a fiction author, you need these as a part of your vocabulary development! They are part of your arsenal of weapons to conquer the hearts of your readers.

Be cautious with your use of these words, though. It is possible to overdo it. When that happens, the description is no longer believable. Use power words in the right places and for the right reason. They should connect the reader to the book, nothing more. Limit the number in a description. If you have a 200-word description, 10 to 14 power words should be plenty!

Provide the Solution

The solution brings together the ideas, tips, methods, techniques, or strategies you have shared in your book. You may have a full paragraph, but you want to have one sentence that brings it together. For example, "This book is designed with tested strategies and skills to help you overcome the emotional stress and social problems associated with being overworked."

Show and Tell Descriptions

I wish Amazon still allowed images to be used in the descriptions. This could work well for fiction, and sometimes for nonfiction too. When you write a description, you should want the reader to visualize an overwhelming problem followed by an incredible, easy solution. This can become an easy formula for either the first or last sentence in the description:

How to (solve the problem) without (difficult solution). For example: "How to lose 100 pounds this year without any rigorous exercise!" Or, "How to increase your income by $20,000 this year, without leaving your current job."

Action Steps:

1) Read your first sentence. Is that the most motivational sentence in the description? How can that sentence be changed to give it more emotional impact?

2) How does your first paragraph increase the reader's desire to know what the book can do for him/her?

3) How does the paragraph summarize the value of the book?

Step 8: Listing the Benefits That Will Rock Your Readers' World

"Sell the sizzle, not the steak." Elmer Wheeler in Tested Sentences That Sell

Help your potential readers to imagine a better future if only they read and apply what you teach in the book. I've read several books on visualization techniques to help me reach goals. This is a variation on that. You lead your readers into visualizing the changes they want just as if they had happened already. More on that in just a moment.

Nonfiction authors should organize benefits in bullet points. Readers are far more likely to read these brief points. A bulleted list can look like this:

- Benefit #1

- Benefit #2

- Benefit #3

On a few, rare occasions, when a series of steps are involved, you could list the benefits numerically, like these:

1. Benefit #1

2. Benefit #2

3. Benefit #3

Your readers will want to know the payoff for getting and reading your book. If you have a good cover and title, they are guessing what is included in the book. The description gives you a chance to remove doubts and to make them see your book as more valuable. Use the list of benefits to show them how wonderful their lives will become if they read and apply the powerful tips in your book. Use your imagination to select which benefits your readers will most enjoy.

If you have a street team of beta readers for your books, notice every favorable comment they make on your advance copy. Ask them what they liked best about the book and what benefits it gave them. Sometimes, those statements will make good bullet points to include in your book description.

Help Readers Visualize the Benefits

I love how Kevin Kruse portrays this stage in writing a book description. He asks us to think, "What if?" and "Just imagine." I like combining his approach with a follow-up question. Here is an example. Just imagine being able to complete your normal weekly workload in just four hours. What could you do with that extra time?

Just imagine being able to complete writing a best-selling book in just seven days. If you could do that, how many books could you write this year? How much might that increase your income?

Just imagine being able to double your car's gas mileage for less than $100. How much money can that save you each year?

What if you could learn to speak conversational Spanish in just 30 days? How could that impact your relationships with people in your community? How could it impact your career?

I could continue with more examples, but you should have the idea by now.

Add Value to Your Book

Consider adding free bonuses to your book. This could be a short report, a checklist, an audio or video download, a newsletter, or a free copy of the next book in a series. Besides increasing the value of your book, it will allow you to add more people to your mailing list. I recommend that you do something such as this for every book you write.

I encourage you to announce this bonus with an emphasized, bold font in your book description. Don't make the bonus a surprise hidden in the book. Make it an extra benefit for those who buy it. If you are putting a priority on list building, you might want to make sure that it appears in the first 10% of the book so that readers can see it in the "Look Inside" feature, even if they don't buy the book. At least, you have another subscriber to contact later.

Amazon offers a wonderful promotion plan called a Kindle Countdown Deal. It includes a countdown timer underneath the price of the book. That timer lets readers know that the price will increase at a specific time and date.

Without a timer and without using up one of the KDP Select promotions, you can change your description to add pressure to buy. It can say something such as: "This introductory offer will expire at midnight on March 31, 2016." This creates a sense of urgency. It can cause them to think, "Either I buy now, or I'll miss this deal!

Tell a Story and Stop

Fiction authors need to work on telling a story in three or four sentences. Then, end the paragraph with a tease! Again, here's an example: "Devin waited, holding her breath. He was so close she could hear his bare feet on the carpet and smell the drying blood on his clothes. He couldn't see her. Should she run? No? Then, what?"

Summary

If you only had 30 seconds to tell a potential reader why they should buy your latest book, what might you say? A book description should take around that long to read. If you haven't captured the reader's interest by that time, they are unlikely to buy the book.

In just a few seconds, your task is to tease and intrigue your readers so they click that "buy button." If they delay too much, you lose. Design your descriptions to sell the product in a hurry. In most cases, "less is more" when sales are involved. Cut your description to the bare minimum, but make it motivating!

Action Steps:

   1)   List three or four ways your readers will have a better life if they read your book.

   2)   List two ways that your book is different and better than

its competitors. If you don't think it is better, maybe it's time to get a good developmental editor!

3) Write one sentence that tells why your book is worth its price tag?

Step 9: How to Write a Call to Action

"If a train is coming at you, closing your eyes won't save you ... but if you look right at it, you at least have a chance to jump." — Andrew Vachss

That is what I mean by a "call to action."
-- Dr. Gary Webb

◆━━━━◆◆━━━━◆━━━━◆◆━━━━◆

No book description is complete without closing the sale with a call to action. Ask for the sale! For readers who have made it to the end of your description, tell them to buy your book!

The Bible says, "You have not because you ask not." This verse applies to prayer, but its principle also applies to sales. The most common and most serious failure of new salespersons is failing to ask the customer to act on the offer we've made.

In email marketing, the two most basic elements of getting a sale are: first, a call to action and secondly, a purchase link. That is why you should consider ways to ask for the sale. You should also pepper your emails with two or more purchase links. Make them stand out so the customer has no problem finding them.

A Call-To-Action (CTA) is essential to every sales email. If you do not have one, don't pretend you want sales! It's that crucial.

Some Examples of Calls to Action

Here are some examples that can be used on your book details page or other sales venues.

1) ACT NOW! Click the link above to get your copy at once. (Link to book sales page).

2) DON'T DELAY! This is a limited time offer. BEST VALUE. Click **HERE**!

3) Offer expires March 1ST. Do NOT miss this! Go to (link) and click the BUY button now!

4) To place your order for _____, click the Buy Now button on **THIS** (hyper-link) Amazon page.

5) START NOW! You can tell this book is a life-changer. BUY IT NOW so you can read and apply these amazing principles in your own life.

6) DOWNLOAD NOW! All you need to do is click the BUY NOW button HERE (insert link). Then, you can immediately read _____ (book title) on your Kindle device, smartphone, tablet or computer. You need not own a Kindle. Get a free app for your computer of device **HERE**. (http://amzn.to/1o0a6Ol)

7) CLICK **HERE** to go to the Amazon page where you can learn more about _____. See what others are saying about this simple, but very helpful book. Then, you can read it at once when you click the BUY button at the top of the page.

8) FOR A SHORT TIME ONLY! This book is on a Kindle Countdown Deal. The price will soon increase. Before that

happens, save money by clicking **HERE**.

9) **ONLY 4 DAYS LEFT!** Sales have been going great, but it is time to go back to the regular price. DO NOT WASTE ANOTHER MINUTE! Get your copy NOW! Click the link below: _____ (Link to book sales page).

10) HURRY! This free promotion was only for three days. Time is running out! Get your copy NOW! Click this link NOW! (Link to book sales page).

11) Let's do this! You know you've been searching for a book like this one. So let's get it done! Click **HERE** (hyperlink the word) to BUY NOW!

12) IT IS FREE TODAY! What have you got to lose? Click the link below so you can read _____ (book title) right now!

13) DON'T HESITATE! This special offer expires today. If you don't BUY NOW, you'll forget, and you'll be sorry! Click **HERE** to go to Amazon and buy _____!

14) BE AWESOME! Learn the secrets tips and techniques in _____ today! Click the link below to read the book and see what I mean! (Link to book sales page)

15) WAITING FOR THE PERFECT TIME? That time is now! Get your (free) copy of _____ before this offer closes. Click the link below to save ___%. (Link to book sales page)

16) WANT A FREE COPY? You won't be able to get it tomorrow! Get your copy RIGHT NOW! Click the link below to buy ___

and immediately read.   (Link to book sales page)

Your book description can become the foundation for selling books through emails, social media posts or through a fan page on Facebook. You can also use it for a book or author web page.

Ways to Accent the Purchase Links

1)   Insert a BUY NOW! button on your web page just beneath your call to action. Then, hyperlink it to the book sales page. This makes it easy for buyers to respond to your offer.

2)   Use color and bold typeface to keywords in the CTA.

3)   Use different and strong fonts. **Arial Black looks very different from plain Arial for example.**

4)   Use a small image of the book as the Click Here link.   Just insert the image into the message body.   Then, highlight or select the image and link it to the book sales page URL.

5)   Use the list subscriber's name at the front of the CTA. Say something like, "Hey Bill, don't waste another moment. This is the book you need! Click the link below to download your copy NOW."

There are plenty of ideas for Calls To Action. I recommend that you sign up for the email lists of great author/book promoters such as Steve Scott, Steve Windsor, Patrick King, and others.   Watch how they word and format their emails.

When you see an effective email, make a copy of it. Another good idea is to adapt it to promote one of your books.   Keep that copy until your next book promotion.

Action Steps:

1) Look at the last two sentences of your description. Do you TELL the reader what they should do? I'm not talking about suggesting it; do you tell them to buy the book? You aren't in an eye-to-eye conversation so it is hard to just ask for the sale. Tell them to buy -- now!

2) Does the sentence before your call to action give a smooth transition from the previous paragraph?

3) If you see part of the sentence you would like to emphasize, put it in a bold font right now. We will look at how to format it later, but this will make you remember to focus your reader's attention on those words.

Step 10: Edit Your Book Description - Some Self Edits and Recommended Tools

"Writing is not like painting where you add. It is not what you put on the canvas that the reader sees. Writing is more like a sculpture where you remove, you eliminate in order to make the work visible. Even those pages you remove somehow remain."
-- Elie Wiesel

＊━━━━━＊＊━━━━━＊━━━━━＊＊━━━━━＊

Readers judge a book by its cover, but also by the quality of its description. If the description is written poorly and filled with ignorant mistakes, it hurts the author's reputation and the book's sales.

I've seen too many book descriptions filled with spelling errors, punctuation errors and grammatical errors. It made the author look ignorant. Who wants to buy a book from a dummy? The solution is to have someone with ability in your topic read through the book description. Then, have someone sharp in grammar read and edit it. Make sure your description doesn't get too long. Even though many writers recommend only 150-200 words, I am more generous. As long as the description is interesting, I allow more if it leads to a strong conclusion and call to action. Here are a few basics on how to edit your book description.

1. Give it a rest. Set the description manuscript aside for 24 hours. Even when that isn't possible, take a break, do something else to clear your head, and come back to it with a fresh perspective. Read the complete description one time. Then, read through it again, looking for how to improve the order of its ideas. Think of it this way; if the description was a list which ideas should be at the top, in the middle, and at the bottom. This should give the material a linear, logical sequence easy for readers to follow.

2. Make it easy. As you read, note any place where the wording causes you to stumble. If you have the manuscript printed, you can do it with a red pen. If on your computer, you might highlight that part in yellow. The wording may be out of order in the sentence. It may be so dull that your mind shifts attention away from the text. Phrases such as those, even whole sentences, may need to be cut or revised. Do not fix it now. Keep reading so you don't lose track of how the story or content is organized. Freely cut sentences or words that are unnecessary.

3. Be alert to your own word quirks. We are creatures of habit. All authors repeatedly make the same grammar, spelling, or punctuation errors when they write. In fact, we are repetitive in using certain favorite words. Rather than trying to give you a list of the most frequently misused or overused words, I'll refer you to Mignon Fogarty's *Grammar Girl's Quick and Dirty Tips for Better Writing*.[2] I have a tendency to use the word "just" too much and in the wrong way. Part of that comes from using it so much when I speak. Since I know I have that problem, I can use the FIND feature in Scrivener or Word to locate every time that word is used. If it is unnecessary, I can delete it. If another word would be clearer, I can replace it.

3. Does it sound right? Be sure to read your book description out loud. Since I use Scrivener software to do my writing, I have the program read the description for me. If I have something misspelled or out of place the software makes it stand out. Hearing the description also helps me detect how the content flows. In addition, listening helps me spot it when paragraphs are out of place.

4. Keep it short and sweet. Authors love words, especially their own. We pile up a mountain of words to explain something we could have said with two or three. Author Stephen King's formula for editing is challenging. He says that the second draft should be 10% less than the first draft.[3] That means 10% of this great writer's text is whittled away by editing and revision. Do you think your first draft is better than his?

Here are a few ideas on how to shorten your book manuscript:
   a)   Cut some of the adverbs, including those with "ly" endings. Ask, "Is that word necessary?"
   b)   Use fewer adjectives. Avoid using them in a series. I'm afraid I'm guilty of that one!
   c)   Gerunds. You may not have heard that word since elementary school if ever. Gerunds are nouns with "ing" added. Instead of saying, "Let's go dancing at the club" you could say, "Let's dance at the club."
   d)   Passive voice. Try not to over-use words the "to be" verbs such as "was," "were," or the word "that." Sometimes these produce an unclear subject in the sentence.
   e)   Description. I'm writing a book on writing book descriptions, but I need to tell you to not use too much description. Use words in ways that allow readers to use their imagination.

5. Use the basic rules of grammar. I realize most of us have not had our grammar closely graded since we were in school. Even college professors are often lenient when they grade our papers. But, you cannot expect your readers to be so indifferent about books they have bought with their own money. Every grammar error has the potential to make your writing harder to understand on a first reading. If your readers spot your errors in grammar, they may question your authority to write. They may consider you less informed than they are. If you are planning to write many books or book descriptions, I recommend that you get a copy of the Chicago Manual of Style or the less expensive McGraw-Hill Handbook of English Grammar and Usage.[4]

6. Don't assume you know the rules of punctuation. A few rules have changed in recent years. Here are a few punctuation rules that are different from what I learned in school.

a) Only leave one space after each form of punctuation, including ones at the end of a sentence. I learned this while editing a book. I will need to go through this book to remove the extra space after periods or other punctuation at the end of a sentence.

b) When I was in school, the English handbooks told us that we were to separate a series of three or more words, but to omit the comma for the last item in the series. Today a series of three or more words always uses a comma to separate the different parts. Here is a strange example though. John ate bologna, crackers and cheese, and grapes. Did you spot it? The writer considers "Crackers and cheese" as one food item in the series. He did not put a comma after crackers because that separates the crackers and cheese as two different items.

7. A professional warning. I am repeating this because it is important. Make the book description appear as though written by the publisher instead of the author. That gives the descriptions more clout or influence. It looks less biased.

8. These are tips for editing your own work. That does not mean you shouldn't get another set of eyes on your writing. If you don't have an editor friend, you can get someone on fiverr.com to look it over for $5. If that seems too steep, ask two or more friends to read it. Ask one to look for spelling and English errors. Ask another what could be done to make the book seem more valuable.

Tools to Help with Editing Your Book

No editing software will take the place of someone skilled with the language and very organized in how they approach the way a book or passage is organized. No author can approach his own book with complete objectivity. We have blind spots because we overlook our most common writing problems.

Authors need to learn to use a few of the most common kinds of editing software. Using it will save a great deal of money when you hire an editor at an hourly rate. It will also help you set up a long-term relationship with an editor who trusts the consistent quality of your manuscripts. This can save you money. Some of the tools I recommend are free; some, inexpensive; and some are costly. They are a good investment for authors who intend to publish more books.

Word Frequency Counter. If you have problems using the same words too often, this app will help you spot them. It is a free online program.

ProWritingAid. You can use this amazing software for free up to 19 times. If you want to buy, it will only cost $35 per year. It even has a desktop version for Macs and Scrivener! I love it!

Grammarly. This online grammar and spelling checker can also be added to Google Chrome to edit posts online such as on social media. It has a paid version too.

Hemingway Editor. This app simplifies your writing if you are prone to writing complicated sentences. Many short pieces such as book descriptions are hard to understand because the sentences are too long. The online version if free to use, but the desktop version only costs $9.99.

Action Steps:

1) Read your description headline. What emotions does it stir? Does it shock? Stir curiosity? Make you laugh? Bottom line: could it make readers hit that "Read more" link to find out what you have to say?

2) How many words are in your longest sentence? If over ten words, try to make it shorter. Does your description include questions and direct statements? Try to use both for variety.

3) Run the spelling and grammar check in your word processing software. Don't blindly accept every suggestion

unless you know it is right.

4) If you know that you are often repetitive or incorrect in your use of specific words, you can do a "find" search with your word processing software to locate those words. Fix any that can be stated better.

5) If your grammar is weak, run the free online version of Grammarly. If you tend toward making your sentences too complex, use the free Hemingway app to improve the simplicity of your description.

6) Ask someone else to read your description. Then ask them whether it makes them more curious or more interested in your book. Ask them if they see something that needs to be improved.

Step 11: How to Format Your Description to Motivate Reader/Buyers

The way a book description looks also matters. On Amazon, through KDP, it's possible to format the description to make it more appealing.
-- Sabrina Ricci

Formatting a book description comprises two parts, both of them are done after the text is written. First, be sure that the order of the content is right. Second, make the description's appearance emphasize what you want the reader to know and feel.

Set the Content in Order

Hopefully, you completed most of this work when you went through the editing phase. However, you should review it as you add the appearance features.

Your goal is to arrange each sentence and paragraph so it builds on the earlier statements and leads the buyer to be ready to respond to the call to action.

Here is a suggested five-step pattern for structuring a nonfiction book description:
1) Headline
2) Engaging the reader with the problem/need to be addressed in the book.
3) Benefits (Bullet points recommended)
4) Closing. Qualify the buyer. Help the reader be sure

this book is the right one for his/her needs.
5)   Call to action.

We have already discussed every part of a description of these except the closing. You want to use the closing to get everyone who might enjoy the book to buy it.

Varied Text Formatting

As stated earlier, I don't begin my book descriptions with the main headline. I wish Amazon would return to their earlier book page layout. In the past, their book detail pages showed more of the description and included the orange <h2> headlines that captured reader attention.

Since they had these changes, I now start with large, bold typeface saying, "**BOOK DESCRIPTION**." This makes the book description much more visible to readers skimming the page. Here is how I began the description for my previous book:

BOOK DESCRIPTION
Do you know how to get more and better book reviews during the first week of your launch?

Within the pages of this book, you'll discover how to navigate past Amazon's rigid terms of service to get quality reviews that get more sales.
Read more

Not every best-selling author uses the same approach. Some authors begin by repeating the book title in large <h1> or <h2> tags like I did at first (you'll understand that better later in the chapter). Here is how Mike Fishbein did his:

How To Self-Publish Amazon Kindle eBooks That Actually Sell

Don't Waste Your Time Writing a Book That Nobody Buys...

Are you looking to grow your business and income through self-publishing a book? Ready to boost your brand and become a bestselling author?

He redeemed himself with a good first sentence, but that sentence could have made a great headline.

Others launch right into the description by using an extra large headline <h1>. Here is an example from Steve Windsor's book description for his book *9 Day Novel Self Publishing:*

Self Publishing is Hard?!

Does the **KDP dashboard** feel like the control panel of a jumbo jet?

Does getting your book **self published to CreateSpace** feel like

▾ Read more

I like Steve's approach. It stands out enough that readers are likely to hit the "Read more" link. That's the whole point of these first few lines.

Steve's partner, Lise Cartwright is a good friend for all self-published authors.   She has helped me with several book promotions a few years back.   She also has great insight into the psychology and structure of book descriptions.   Because of that, I recommend that you read her blog post at http://bit.ly/1TtNe9c.

Make Your Description More Attractive with HTML Tags

When you input a book description into Kindle Direct Publishing's Bookshelf or into the Createspace Dashboard, you will only produce a plain text description on Amazon. There will be no bold, italic, or underlined text. All the text all will be the same size. Carriage returns or paragraph breaks are inconsistent. That's why it is important for you to learn a few basic HTML tags to control how your text looks.

As I said earlier, I wish Amazon had not eliminated the orange headlines. I understand why they did it, but I also think it weakened our ability to attract readers to the description. Now, you must learn to use a few combinations of HTML tags to create an intense emphasis for your headlines and main headings. Now, the heading tags only control the size for the text, not the color. You can see a comparison of sizes for various the heading tags at http://bit.ly/1cB78J2

HTML format tags often begin with < > and end with </ >. For example, <h2> This is a second level heading.</h2> The <h2> begins the heading and </h2> closes out that format. These same symbols are used with other tags too.

Amazon does not accept all HTML codes, but they allow enough to make your descriptions attractive.

I use an online tool called real-time HTML editor. You can find and use it at http://bit.ly/1gNxKel. It has a split screen. The top one is where you insert the HTML coded text. The lower one is how your description will look when it shows up on Amazon. To help you see how it works, let's try an experiment together.

Go to the top section of the HTML editor. Delete the existing text. Then, copy and paste the following text into the upper section. See how it looks!

––––––––––––––––

<h2>BOOK DESCRIPTION</h2> <b>BOOK REVIEWS THAT SELL: Discover the Secrets of Getting a Boatload of Great Reviews</b><p>Having a good number of high-quality book reviews can make the difference between mediocre books sales and having a best seller. Dr. Webb's last four books have ranked #1 in their categories. </p><p><b>Even after such success, Dr. Webb recognized that he was neglecting an important part of maintaining long-term sales.</b> He concentrated on getting about 15-20 reviews immediately following the release of his books, but he failed to establish the process for getting more and better reviews, setting higher goals for reviews after the book launch. <b>His research and testing for this book will prove themselves within the first week of launch, but also for the extended period following its initial success.</b></p><p></p><h3>By reading <i>BOOK REVIEWS THAT SELL</i>, you will learn:</h3><ul><li>Reasons why Amazon may soon remove some of your best reviews.</li><li>Techniques and tips for increasing the quality and quantity of reviews you are getting.</li><li>How to recognize the most common mistakes authors are making when seeking more reviews.</li><li>A system for identifying and tracking actual and potential reviewers for your books.</li><li>A legitimate way to use

virtual assistants to help increase the number of reviews you get.</li><li>How to screen potential reviewers to avoid the harshest and most negative ones.</li><li>How to best handle the inevitable one-star review.</li><li>How to build a large pool of reviewers who will be glad to see another book released with your name on it.</li><li>How to have reviewers contacting you, asking for a review copy of your next book.</li></ul><h3>The key to book sales is through building a relationship with your readers. But, did you know that the key to getting more and better reviews is establishing ways to communicate better with existing and potential reviewers?</h3>Read this simple, little book to find out the strategies, systems, and skills involved in building a reliable, long-term network of reviewers. Learn how to establish a sense of scarcity among your reviewers so that they pursue you instead of the other way around.<h3>ACT NOW! Click that orange BUY button at the top of this page.</h3>Then, you'll be able to develop your system to collect high-quality reviews by the boatload. You'll be able to immediately read <b><i>BOOK REVIEWS THAT SELL: Discover the Secrets of Getting a Boatload of Great Reviews</i></b> on your Kindle device, laptop, tablet, or smartphone.

It may take some practice to get everything right, but you can always change this sample description.

Remember to use <b> and <u> combinations or <h2> and <u> combinations to make words or sentences stand out and to separate sections of the description.

A well-done HTML description can help make yours stand out

above your competition.

Here is the complete list of HTML codes that will work in KDP book descriptions:

<b> Bold </b>

<em>

<font>

<h1> Headline 1st Level

<h2> Headline 2nd Level (Remember that <h2> no longer is orange)

<h3> Headline 3rd Level

<h4> Headline 4th Level

<h5> Headline 5th Level

<h6> Headline 6th Level

<hr>

<i> Italics

<li> List (used in combination with <ol> or <ul>

<ol> Ordered List (Numbered List)

<p> Paragraph, new one

<pre>

<s> Strikethrough

<strike> Strikethrough

<strong>

<sub> Subscript

<sup> Superscript

<u> Underline

<ul> Unordered List (Bulleted List)

To make lists, you will need to decide if you want it to be a numbered list or a bulleted one. Numbered lists are ordered lists that start with <ol> and end with </ol>. Bulleted lists begin with <ul> and end with </ul>. The numbers or bullets are entered when you insert the <li> and </li> tags. Here is how that looks:

Here is a list of benefits from your book:
<ul><li>bullet 1
<li>bullet 2
<li> bullet 3</ul>

Paste that into the html editor to see how it looks when converted to real text format.

Tools for Formatting Book Descriptions

In the past, I have shown you how to use the online real-time HTML editor http://bit.ly/1gNxKel to format your book description.

Years ago, I bought another small piece of software for formatting book descriptions. The **Book Description Editor** is no longer being sold, but I found it online for free at http://dlcom.co/1mWXVoz. Since Amazon changed away from the orange headlines after this tool was created, those still appear in the software. However, when the description is uploaded to KDP, the orange color isn't used. So, it still works well for beginners.

Another free tool can be found at http://kindlepreneur.com/amazon-book-description-generator/. This is an online tool that will need practice before you are producing excellent formatting for your descriptions.

I think using these tools and then studying the code that is produced can help you learn the basic HTML coding that you need.

Soon, you won't even need the tools at all.

Additional Sources to Learn How to Use HTML

Please understand that many of these have not adjusted to Amazon's change that doesn't produce an orange headline when you use <h2> headers. Don't worry about the color. It just doesn't appear on Amazon. It is still the same <h2> tag.

https://understandinge.com/amazon-html-product-descriptions/

http://fixmystory.com/2015/03/03/how-to-make-your-amazon-description-stand-out/

http://bookmarketingtools.com/blog/how-to-format-your-kindle-book-descriptions-with-html/

Action Steps:

1) Open the real-time HTML editor at http://bit.ly/1gNxKel. Delete the text in the upper section of the split screen. Then, copy and paste your book description into that section. Use the HTML codes listed above and see how they change the look of the text in the lower section.   Experiment with changes until your description has the effect you want.

2) When you finish step #1, copy the contents of the upper section of the screen and paste them into the book description box in the KDP Bookshelf.

Step 12: How to Upload Your Description to KDP and/or Createspace

"Your description can be perfect, but first it must be seen."
-- Dr. Gary Webb

━━━━━━━━━━━━━━━━━━━━━━━━━━

At last, you've gotten your description written and formatted. One task remains -- getting it active on Amazon. While valuable for the back cover of a printed book the description doesn't show automatically on the Amazon book page. The description is also great for your promotional emails and social networking, but I'm sure most of you are primarily concerned with getting it on Amazon or other retail sites.. For Amazon, the description must be uploaded through KDP Bookshelf, Createspace Dashboard, or through Author Central.

Kindle Direct Publishing

Let's begin with the assumption you have not published your book previously on KDP. But, you can use the same approach when revising a description after the book is published.

When you upload your book to Kindle Direct Publishing through its Bookshelf, you add the book by clicking the "Create new title" link at the top of the Bookshelf main page.

You are then taken to the first of two data entry pages.

In section one, you will enter the book details such as the title, subtitle, publisher, author, etc. The book description entry box is where you should paste your description. I say that because you should have your description written and formatted before getting to this point. Be careful that you have copied the correct HTML coded text before you paste it into this box because it takes 12-72 hours for it to be processed by KDP. During that time, you cannot see how it will look on Amazon. In addition, you cannot make changes if you have overlooked something.

Be sure to check your description as soon as it goes live on Amazon. Be sure it has no errors and that its appearance features are what you wanted.

Createspace

If you haven't already published your book, click the "Add New Title" button on the Dashboard to start. After you've added the title and type of project, you can start by choosing to use the guided or expert setup. The description is one of the final things to enter. This is located in the distribution section.

You are allowed a maximum of 4000 characters. Advanced users may use a list of HTML tags that is more limited than what is used for Kindle Direct Publishing.

Here are the ones allowed[5]:

Allowed Tags

Text Style Tags
`<b>` or `<strong>`
`<i>` or `<em>`
`<font>` (align, color, and face)
`<pre>`
`<s>` or `<strike>`
`<sub>`
`<sup>`
`<u>`

Formatting Tags
`<p>`
`<br>`
`<ol>`, `<ul>`, and `<li>`

Using Author Central to Enter Book Descriptions

After you have submitted your book to Kindle Direct Publishing, you may shift to Author Central for making any future modifications to the book description. Do not go back and forth between Author Central and KDP because it will create confusion. Differences in the allowed tags and how they are processed will create problems.

One of the interesting advantages of using Author Central is its built-in HTML book description editor. It has two separate tabs, one for composing text and the other to see its HTML. You can see that below:

COMPOSE   EDIT HTML

Format: **B** *I* ☰☷

BOOK DESCRIPTION

Do You Know the 12 Proven Steps To Write Book Descriptions to Make Your Book Sell?
Nonfiction authors often neglect being creative when writing book descriptions.
They imagine that the great content inside the book will make it a success. What a joke!

Observe the four options available in the "compose" mode. It offers bold text, italics, numbered and bulleted lists. To use other features, you will need to shift to the HTML tab.

Under the HTML tab, you can only use the tags allowed for Createspace. Notice that Author Central provides a Preview feature that allows you to see how it will appear in Amazon.

Action Steps:

1) If you have not added your book to KDP, do so now. Sign in to kdp.amazon.com and click on the Bookshelf tab. Click "Create New Title" like you see below.

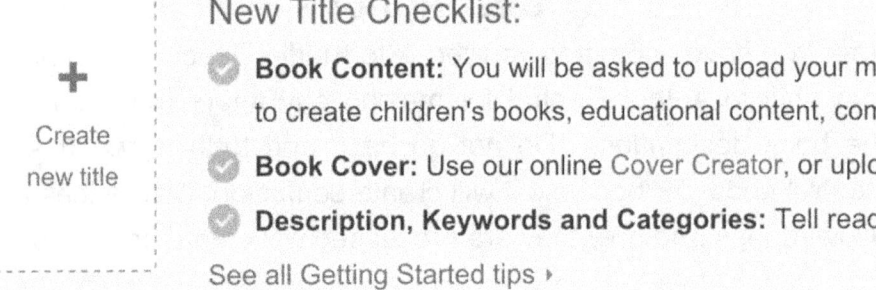

2) You should now be using the set-up portion of Bookshelf. The HTML book description should be pasted into the fifth data box in section 1. Notice the 4000-character limit. That limit should be no problem because 4000 characters equal over 500 words. Notice that the entry box can be expanded by clicking and holding down the lower right corner. This should allow you to see all the text that is entered.

Description (What's this?)

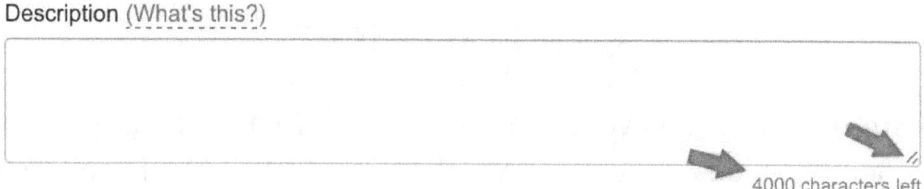

4000 characters left

3) Paste the HTML coded book description into this block. Finish entering the other data on the page, save and continue to finish the second page. I copy my description straight from the real-time HTML editor in my browser. Never do your coding in MS Word because it has hidden HTML codes that might your descriptions formatting properly in KDP or in Createspace.

Conclusion

I am thankful you have purchased and used this book to prepare better book descriptions. As of March 2016, this information reflects the current standards set by Amazon. But, these standards often change. If you notice a problem with how Amazon processes your description, please contact me at gary@mgwebb.net.

I will help you with the specific problem and will update the book to show any changes by Amazon.

Appendix A: Most Common Mistakes with Book Descriptions

Authors make two great mistakes when writing their book descriptions. Sometimes they write too much; at other times, they write too little. Giving too much information on the book makes buying unnecessary. Sharing too little makes buying unlikely.

So what should a writer include in an effective book description? As I will share later, the broad genre will decide the answer.

Fiction books should show the genre of the book. Is it historical fiction, romance, a thriller, mystery, paranormal fantasy, etcetera? Is it a vampire novel? A Christian romance (big market right now).

Nonfiction books should state the particular niche. It could be weight loss or fitness. Or self-help. What about business and marketing? Or beauty care? Or hunting and fishing? The options are an endless array of human interests and concerns.

For fiction, you need to arouse the curiosity of readers while still hinting at the benefits. Sometimes, simple questions can be used.

Your aim is not to hoodwink readers into buying books they will hate. Write descriptions to get the right readers to buy the right book for their needs. If you get the wrong readers to buy your book, you'll both regret it.

Be careful not to overuse superlatives. That includes statements such as, "This is the best romantic comedy you'll ever read." That may be true, but it gives no convincing information about this book. Instead, use power words such as shocking, terrifying, exciting, sexy, hilarious, thrilling, or fierce. These are words that stir emotions and may influence purchases.

Don't use long, complex sentences. Make each sentence count and make it stand out. One way to do that is by breaking the text into short paragraphs. A one-sentence paragraph is enough. This technique creates white space framing the key ideas. It is a bracketing effect, making the sentence stronger.

Five Common Problems with Book Descriptions

Failure to edit the description. A book description containing poor grammar, misspelled words, and terrible punctuation is a negative advertisement for the book. It proclaims the author either does not know basic English or doesn't care for his readers. Many authors lack technical writing skills and depend on editors to correct their mistakes. But, readers don't even care about that. They pay for value received, so they depend on the description to showcase the author's writing ability. An unedited book description signals potential readers to not bother getting the book. The book may be just as bad as the description!

Failure to limit what you include. Tell the potential reader enough to motivate them to buy. No more! Do not give away the surprise ending to your thriller or too much of the advice in your self help book. Use the book description to tease readers with the possibilities of what is inside the book. Do not make buying it unnecessary. Your description should be like an appetizer instead of a meal. An appetizer doesn't satisfy our hunger; it whets our appetite. Let your description stir the reader's desire to find out just how good your book is.

Failure to identify the audience you expect to help. Be sure to answer the question: "Who could benefit the most from reading this book?" Believe me, you don't want to risk having your book fall into the hands of disappointed readers. No matter how good your book is, it is not for everyone. You should want none of your readers to feel cheated. Money from one sale cannot replace the income lost because of a bad review. Your book description should motivate the readers who later will be glad they bought it.

Failure to show how the book might benefit its readers. Don't just tell what information the book contains. Your nonfiction book description should not read like a table of contents. That is not good advertising. Your book description should persuade the reader to buy. It does that by painting a picture of how their lives will be better after they read and apply the book's ideas. Even a novel should deliver benefits such as inspiration, entertainment, excitement,. Nonfiction books should teach how to change the reader's thoughts, skills, and behavior. After reading your book on wedding photography, how will readers benefit? Maybe it will help them capture memories that happy couples will treasure for a lifetime. Your book on bass fishing may put that gold trophy on the mantle when they win the next big tournament.

Failure to ask for the sale. Here is where most new salesmen fail. They do a good job presenting the product, but then they fail to ask the potential customer to buy. They fail to guide the customer into how to complete that sale and make the product their own.

Many authors think it's ridiculous to tell customers how to buy. I don't. I tell them to scroll to the top of the page and click the orange "buy button" on Amazon. I don't want them to get distracted before they make the buy. I want them to feel an urgency to act now. Then, they can get the benefits I've told them are in the book.

Appendix B: How to Enhance Fiction Book Descriptions

The Structure of a Fiction Book Description

The first sentence of most book descriptions for novels include the name and some key perspective on the main character. Following sentences should cause us to know why we should like or hate that character.

Early sentences should expose us to the essential conflict or point of tension within the plot. What is the confronting problem(s) that he is striving to overcome (even if he is an evil force you instantly despise). Describe the point of pain that the character feels in words that cause your readers to have a visceral connection.

Know the Basic Types of Fiction Books

Many fiction readers know what they like in terms of a specific category like science fiction, horror, suspense, romance, historical fiction, or crime. Each of these has a distinct writing style, plot design, and character set.

Besides these genres, there are other factors that hold the loyalty of readers. Some readers love to read "regency romance." These are novels set during the period of the British Regency of the early 19th century (1811-1820). Even this niche has its subdivisions. Traditional regency romance novels unfold with a focus on historical accuracy regarding the values and historical minutiae of the period. Historical regency romance novels are set in the physical time period, but it includes much more modern elements including explicit sensuality.

You can read an extensive list of definitions for fiction categories and genres at http://bit.ly/1PHabUZ.

Since fiction readers are forced to think of the exact category and type of books they enjoy, you can use those terms in your description to help them quickly identify your book as a possibility. You should also include the term(s) in your metadata description in KDP and Createspace.

It is also helpful to give the time and general location in which the story is set.

One good idea for a fiction book description is to give a small excerpt from the book. Try to select a few lines that leave a character or situation hanging in the air with suspense or curiosity. If your book is filled with humor, spotlight a snippet from a particularly funny portion.

Fiction is powerful in its portrayal of human emotion. Be sure that your description also uses emotional power words to communicate the mood of the story and to hook the heart of the reader. As a reminder, emotional power words make you connect with specific feelings (terrified, teeth-rattling, vicious, horrifying, sizzling, gut-wrenching, devastating, tantalizing, fierce, majestic).

If the book has endorsements from well-known people, especially famous authors, these can lend strength to its message.

Don't give away the plot or the main conflict that drives the characters. Avoid introducing any subplots at all. Stay focused.

Stir questions instead of giving answers.

Quickly introduce your main character without giving background. Write in active, present tense. Show what's happening in a scene. Never merely describe it.

Do NOT give summaries of a chapter, the plot, or the outcome. Don't resort to opening the description with an overused phrase like "In a world where..." Do NOT compare your book with those written by other authors.

Try your best to limit your book description to 150-200 words. I realize that is very challenging when writing a description for a 75-100,000 word novel. I suggest that you try to write out a one-sentence summary of the book to help you keep that focus. This sentence is for your benefit as you write the description. It should not be included in the final version.

Appendix C: Outsourcing

Book Description Writers

Bryan Cohen. http://bryancohen.com/best-page-forward/. 1 Description $97 with copy for Facebook Ad and Landing Page. Rush Order $147. 3-Day Description $197.

Gary Webb. http://mgwebb.net/book-descriptions/. 1 Description: $25. 2 Descriptions: $45. 3 Descriptions: $60. 4 Descriptions: $75. Normal Turn-Around is 3 days or less. **Only for nonfiction books.**

https://www.fiverr.com/russ41burg. $5 per description.

https://www.fiverr.com/conversations/excaliburpress. $5 per description.

Book Editors

https://www.fiverr.com/writerlisaz. If requested, she will edit in Scrivener. That's not easy to find these days.

https://www.fiverr.com/conversations/mrproofreader. He is in high demand, so you must contact him prior to ordering.

http://tahosa.wix.com/tahosaediting. Tahosa Editing. tahosa@enosmills.com, Phone: 970-372-8174. Payment Method: PayPal. Contact name: Eryn Mills. Current charges: $0.005 per word, with a minimum order of $5.00.

Bibliography

Writing Book Descriptions

Green, James. "How to Write an Amazon Book Description" 24hourbestseller.com/how-to-write-an-amazon-book-description/#sthash.iVq3Jwb3.dpuf. January 21, 2015.

Amazon Kindle Book Categories.

Kindlepreneur. "How To Choose The Best Kindle Ebook Categories." http://kindlepreneur.com/how-to-choose-the-best-kindle-ebook-category/.

Using Keywords

Kindle Direct Publishing. "Categories with Keyword Requirements." https://kdp.amazon.com/help?topicId=A200PDGPEIQX41

Kindle Direct Publishing. "Make Your Book More Discoverable with Keywords." https://kdp.amazon.com/help?topicId=A2EZES9JAJ6H02

Kindlepreneur. Amazon Kindle Rankings. http://kindlepreneur.com/amazon-kindle-rankings-2/.

Kindlepreneur. How To Choose The Right Kindle Keywords. http://kindlepreneur.com/how-to-choose-kindle-keywords/

Kindlepreneur. How To Unlock The Secret Kindle Categories. http://kindlepreneur.com/how-to-unlock-the-secret-kindle-categories/

Book Marketing

"98 Book Marketing Ideas." Bookbub Insights. http://insights.bookbub.com/book-marketing-ideas/?utm_source=98+Book+Marketing+Ideas+-+Authors&utm_campaign=961a81c362-RSS_Email_book-marketing-ideas&utm_medium=email&utm_term=0_af315db9be-961a81c362-30774737

Review Request

The Temptations had many bestselling hits. One of them was "Ain't too Proud to Beg." Let me say that I "ain't too proud to beg" for a review. If you found this book useful and have some sense of the kind of reader who would most benefit from it, I ask you to please take a few moments to leave your rating and comments in the review section on Amazon.

To make things a little easier, this link will take you directly to the review page for this book:

https://www.amazon.com/review/create-review?
ie=UTF8&asin=B019RQG1W8#

You can share anything you think will be useful, but

here are a few suggestions:

✓   What did you like most about this book?

✓   What makes this book different from others you have read?

✓   Did it give you practical ways to apply the information it provides? If so, share what you are going to be doing differently because you read it.

✓   What kinds of readers would benefit most reading this book?

Immediately after reading is the best time to leave a review.

About the Author

If you think you need a high-priced coach/trainer to succeed in your self-publishing career, you might be wrong! Do you:

- Want to know some good writing and research tips for beginning authors?
- Want to better understand how to set up your book on Amazon or Createspace?
- Need help with your book promotion and marketing plans?
- Have questions about Amazon's policies on book reviews and how to get more and better
- reviews?
- What to write better book descriptions?
- Maybe have more specific questions?

Dr. Gary Webb loves authors and wants to help. He does not consider himself a "guru" with all the answers, but his books have become consistent bestsellers in the nonfiction research category. Since he considers this passion to be fun, he normally doesn't charge for his services. He just does it for the fun of it. Who knows? Any coaching session might give an idea for a new book!

Also, he has dabbled with other topics to enhance his experience with fields such as weight loss, personal finances, and religion. His greatest satisfaction is interacting with authors who have read his books and have specific questions remaining.

Gary also enjoys fishing, running, and spending time with his wife, Jane. They have retired to Dalton, Georgia, a community perfect for both of these pastimes.

Other Books You Might Enjoy

Christian Topics

Free Indeed: A Devotional for Saints Who Still Struggle with Sin

The Meaning of the Cross: Its Impact on Your Life

Weight Loss

Lasting Weight Loss: What Have You Got to Lose?

Your 5 Keys to Keeping Weight Off: Answers that Work

Self-Publishing

Prepare! Publish Promote Books 1-3

Book Reviews That Sell: Discover the Secrets of Getting a Boatload of Great Reviews

Writing Killer Sales Emails: A Step-by-Step Guide

Learn more about these and order them at www.mgwebb.net

---

[1] KDP. "Categories with Keyword Requirements." https://kdp.amazon.com/help?topicId=A200PDGPEIQX41

[2] Mignon Fogarty. *Grammar Girl's Quick and Dirty Tips for Better Writing.* http://www.amazon.com/dp/B002ASFPYQ/

[3] Stephen King, *On Writing.* p. 282

[4] Chicago Manual of Style. http://www.amazon.com/dp/0226104206/.

McGraw-Hill Handbook of English Grammar and Usage, 2nd Edition. http://www.amazon.com/dp/B00924B6I0/

[5] http://www.betterbooktools.com/createspace-html-code-editor/

www.ingramcontent.com/pod-product-compliance
Lightning Source LLC
Chambersburg PA
CBHW070327190526
45169CB00005B/1773